Internet Marketing

Top 10 Most Effective Strategies

Table Of Contents

Introduction

Most traditional ways of marketing suit big businesses. For small enterprises, internet marketing is a great option. Not only is it cheap, but it also expands your reach. This realization hit me when I had just established my business.

I've always been fascinated with how much you can achieve on the web. And I knew that internet marketing would be my springboard if I was to use it right. But there was a problem - no one was there to show me how to get started with it. Or at least, give me a list of the best strategies to follow.

Still, I forged ahead; determined to succeed regardless of my situation. And when you do something wrong for some time, you finally learn to do it right.

In this book, I will show you the internet marketing strategies that worked for me. Also, I will give you tips on how to get started using them.

Enjoy the reading!

Chapter 1: Create Value

You have a product to sell. That's your motivation for reading this book. If it wasn't for this product, you would be watching TV at the moment.

But there is one thing that must be made clear – if your product has low customer value, you won't make many sales. Success, so to speak, will be a far-fetched dream.

What is Customer Value?

Customer value is the difference between what the customer gains from the product, and what he is willing to give to get it.

You have had the experience before. You buy a product and get it home. After a few hours, you start feeling that you have been ripped off. This is an example of low customer value. Your intuition makes you believe that you overpaid for the product.

Success in the market is a result of high customer value.

The Importance of Customer Value

The significance of creating high customer value cannot be overstated. Every other marketing strategy you can think of depends on it.

No one buys a product; everybody buys a benefit. Would you purchase a Plasma TV if your bedroom already has one? Probably not! Otherwise, the second one would be left to gather dust.

Customers don't want to know what your product is; they want to know what it can do for them. And if the benefits are greater than the cost, that's high customer value. It tells customers the benefits they will get from the product.

Additionally, high customer value creates repeat buys and referrals. This builds trust and brand loyalty, enabling you to sell more.

How to Increase Customer Value

Here are the steps you must follow:

1. Understand the needs of the customers – you can do this by conducting surveys, studying buying trends, and using other research tactics. But before you do this, you must first determine your customers.

2. Analyze competition – these are roadblocks you must overcome to reach your customers. So make it a point to know who your competitors are, what they do, how they do it, and where they do it wrong.

3. Analyze your organization – your other task is to look at your product and determine how well it fulfills your customer's needs.

4. Work on ways of improving customer value – you should now have a better picture of how your market looks. That is, you may now know where the weaknesses are so that you can improve them. Or it may be that you have discovered something your competitors don't have or aren't doing.

In the end, what you want is a win-win situation for you and your customers. They want products that solve their problems at fair prices and you want to charge enough to make a profit. Once you achieve this balance, other online marketing strategies become easy.

Chapter 2: Search Engine Optimization

SEO means making your website attractive to search engines. When done right, your website can rank higher in search results that would increase visits. And these are not just any visits; they represent people interested in your product.

Furthermore, higher rankings are synonymous with being an authority. And this can increase trust in your customers.

How To Start Using SEO

SEO is one complicated subject. And it's only when you get your feet in it that you realize how vast it is. But that should not stop you from knowing the basics. So here they are:

Find keywords – keywords are an important aspect of SEO. They tell search engines what your page is about. For example, "introduction to SEO" will notify search engines that you want to teach beginners about SEO. Without keywords, search engines cannot understand your website. Therefore, they cannot rank it.

When researching keywords, with a tool like Google's Keyword Planner, you must choose high-volume, low competition words. This may sound easy – it's a lot of work but with higher dividends when done right.

The trend is to go for long-tail keywords. These are easy to rank since they have low competition. So instead of going for "affordable hotels," you can opt for "affordable hotels in Hong Kong."

Produce quality content – SEO isn't about stuffing your content with keywords anymore. Those days are gone. Search engines have gotten smarter and practices to fool them will get you penalized. Better rankings will come if you produce great content. This means everything you post on your website must be helpful to people.

Improve user experience – your website must not be heavy to load. It must not put your visitors on a treasure-hunting quest; it needs to be easy to navigate. Search engines watch the friendliness of every website on the net. Those with the worst user experience don't get better rankings.

Have a mobile-friendly website – in one research, 40% of users turned to a competitor's website because the website they first visited was not mobile friendly. The number of people accessing the internet using mobile devices has increased. So if you want to improve your ranking, a mobile-friendly site isn't something you should ignore.

Monitor your results – SEO isn't something you do once and forget. You need to monitor it. If things are not working, you should take remedial action.

Depending on your needs, you may have to hire an SEO expert. But if you are ready to get your hands dirty, then tap into the huge pool of SEO tutorials online. Just know that mastering this subject will take time and hard work.

Chapter 3: Social Media Marketing

Social Media Marketing (SMM) refers to all marketing done on social media sites. The most notable ones include Facebook, Twitter, Pinterest, Instagram, Google Plus+, Tumblr, and LinkedIn. Thanks to advancements in technology, many are now on these websites. This gives you an opportunity to get closer to your customers.

The Importance of SMM

Ignoring social media is one of the worst blunders you can make. Not only will you miss potential sales, but you will also give your competitors an edge. Here are some important points of social media marketing.

Drive traffic to your website – apart from search engines, social media sites are your next bet to increasing your website's traffic. This is important as it may...

Increase your sells – no one visits a website just because he feels like it. There is always a reason. Although some will be there just for information, some will be there to buy.

Strengthens the relationship with your customers – social media allows you to interact with consumers on a personal level.

How To Get Started With SMM

Opening an account on a social media site is easy. The hard part comes when you start building a following. But with dedication, you can do it. Here are some things to keep in mind:

Have a goal – nobody, in his right mind, begins a journey without knowing his destination. The same applies in every SMM campaign. So decide now. Do you want to increase sells? Or do you want to increase brand awareness? Your answer to this question will determine the type of content you will make for your account.

Know where your audience hangs out – you are free to open an account on every social media site in existence. Unfortunately, this will be a burden on your resources (time and money). If your business is small, you should focus on just one or two networking sites. And these must be the ones preferred by your customers.

Create great content – great content is everything on the web. So before you post anything on your social accounts, check its quality. If you find it lacking, improve it.

Have a schedule – you must have a timetable for posting content on your accounts. Inconsistency is a recipe for disaster.

Build followers organically – do not get caught up in the numbers. Ten engaged followers are better than 5,000 bought ones, who don't even know your business's name. So build your followers the traditional way.

Chapter 4: Pay-Per-Click Marketing

SEO is quite effective at generating traffic. Above all, it's free. The only drawback is that it takes time to show results. So if you want traffic quickly, it may not be a good option. This is where PPC comes in.

What Is PPC?

PPC is an acronym for pay-per-click. That is, an ad with search results embedded is placed on a website and you pay for it when a user clicks it. An example is the advertisements you see in Google's search results.

At the heart of PPC is the process of bidding for keywords. Depending on the number of bidders, the price for a click may vary.

But choosing a keyword does not guarantee a ranking. Many factors are taken into account before search engines can start including your ad in search results.

When done correctly, PPC can generate a substantial amount of targeted traffic that will result in better conversions. If you are selling something, you can make a quick profit.

However, PPC can also be a graveyard if not properly planned. It's common to spend money and get nothing in return.

Tips for Successful PPC Campaigns

Just as with SEO, you won't master PPC in a day. It takes time. But if you are work hard at it, you should be running at full speed in no time. Here are things to remember:

Choose the right keywords – this cannot be overemphasized. So give it the attention it deserves. Just as with SEO, you must go for specific, high volume, low competition keywords. These will keep the price per click low while increasing conversions. Going for words like "desks" because it has a high search volume is not smart. "Ergonomic office desks" is less competitive, making it a better option.

Write your ad properly – the words in your ad must persuade customers to click. So take time to make them persuasive.

Focus on conversions – clicks won't make you any money. What you need are conversions. So when your ad goes live, track the number of people answering your call to action.

Monitor and adjust – don't just launch a campaign and forget about it. You must keep on tweaking things. This will increase your chances of success.

Chapter 5: Blogging

Blogging began as a form of a personal diary. With time, people discovered that they could use these platforms profitably. Blogs are now powerful business tools and not just collections of random thoughts.

Blog is the short form of weblog. In essence, it is a special type of a website, but unlike a regular website, a blog is updated regularly. Furthermore, it is interactive giving businesses a chance for two-way communication with customers.

Why Start Blogging?

In the US, 40% of companies use a blog in their marketing campaigns. And this is no surprise, considering that companies that blog get 55% more visits than those that don't. Need more convincing on why you should have a blog? Read on.

Blogs make communicating with customers easy – you can update a blog daily. This is not the case with a website. Additionally, a blog has a commenting system for customers to talk to you.

Helps you understand your customers – apart from social media sites, a blog is another way to stay closer to your customers.

Blog posts are easy to share – sharing content that is on a website is not easy. Much of it is about your product or company. But with blogs, this is not usually the case.

Good for SEO – since blogs are updated regularly, search engines love them. And this increases your traffic.

How To Start a Blog

There are a lot of tips on the internet to get you started with blogging. Gone are the days you needed to be a programmer to develop a good website. Below are some things to help you on your blogging journey.

Determine your audience – this will dictate the type of content you will have on your blog, so don't skimp on this step. A blog is there to serve your product, but at the same time, it must be appealing to your readers. Selling all the time won't do you any good. You must keep a balance between selling and giving readers what they want.

Monitor the competition – you must never lose sight of what the competition is up to. So bookmark all your competitors' blogs.

Keep on making more content – it can be hard to maintain a blog, especially when it's new. However, you must still force yourself to write daily. If you can't, aim for at least three posts per week.

Remember SEO – this must be integrated into your blog. As you read in Chapter 2, it's one of the most effective ways to increase your traffic.

Promote the blog in other channels – if you want to grow your traffic, you must advertise your blog at every chance you get. So have its URL on your business card, car, etc.

Chapter 6: Guest Blogging

Guest blogging is tantamount to getting a spot on somebody's show. If your ideas are great, you can be a star by the end of your session.

When you guest blog, you write a post on someone else's blog. Unlike ghostwriting, the post is published in your name - this has many benefits for your business. Here are some of them:

It gives you exposure – without a name, it can be tough to gain customers in the face of competition. Guest blogging gives you a platform to show what you can do for potential customers.

It generates traffic – a great post will get people's attention. As a result, they will want to know more about you or respond to your call to action.

Great for SEO – in each post, you can put a link or two pointing to your website. These links are called "backlinks". They are like votes for your website. The more of them you have, the better. Search engines use them to determine your rank.

It's a form of networking – aligning yourself with influencers is important in business and Internet marketing is no exception. Networking gives you knowledge about your industry and it also opens new business opportunities.

How to Get Started with Guest Blogging

Guest blogging becomes easy once you lay the groundwork. Here are tips you can follow:

Have a great blog – before you start seeking guest blogging opportunities, you should have a blog of your own. Although this is not mandatory, it makes landing opportunities easy. Other businesses will want to see what you can do before they open their doors to you.

Choose quality blogs – even when you're desperate for customers, you must not settle for less. Guest blogging takes a lot of effort so the results must be worth it. In your quest, you should choose authority blogs. These have a lot of readers. Moreover, the backlinks you will get from them will be quality ones.

Don't be afraid to initiate contact – you should pitch your ideas to editors of blogs you want to write for. Unfortunately, contacting these people is the scariest part of guest blogging. You must know, however, that you have nothing to lose. If you do not get awarded the opportunity, you should be proud that you at least tried.

Go the extra mile – assuming you get a guest-blogging chance, which you will if you work at it, you must work hard to create a great post. You want it to get people's attention. And you also want it to make way for more guest blogging opportunities.

Promote your post – once your post is live, you must take time to make it popular.

Respond to comments – you should respond to people's comments. This is a simple way to build a relationship with them.

Chapter 7: Video Marketing

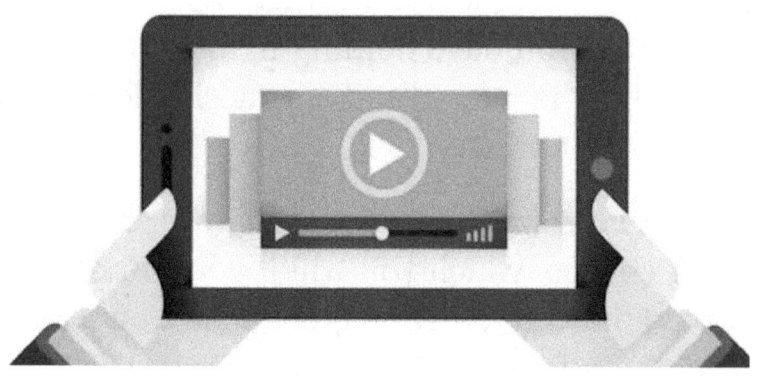

Video marketing is the process of using videos in your marketing campaigns. You may do this to promote products or your company. The use of video marketing has grown in recent years and technology has managed to keep up with it.

Why is Video Marketing Effective?

The popularity of video marketing is no accident. Here are some of the ways it can help your company:

It's great for SEO – websites that use video content achieve better rankings. Search engines like Google have made it clear that they love videos.

Increases conversions – as said earlier, you need conversions and not just clicks. Research showed that 57% of customers are likely to buy after watching a video demonstration of a product.

Video is easy to remember – 80% of information that is seen and heard is remembered but you only recall 20% of things you see. As for things you hear, the percentage drops to 10. So if you want to glue information into your customer's heads, a video is your best option.

How to Get Started

Getting started with video marketing is expensive and time-consuming. You will, of course, need the obvious tools: a camera, a microphone, a pair of headphones, and lights. And you must learn to make good use of these.

Here are some tips for successful video marketing:

Have a purpose – every video you make should have a purpose. Online users have so much on their plates so they don't like getting their time wasted.

Keep them short – longer videos don't always get many views on the internet so you make yours as short as possible. Proper planning before you get in front of the camera is crucial.

Free vs paid hosting – you have a choice to host videos on your own for a fee or upload them on free sites like YouTube. The former directs traffic to your website and gives you more control. But it can take time to gain a following. The latter provides instant traffic. Unfortunately, this traffic goes to the hosting website. So you must decide on what's best for your business.

You can make videos on a range of topics. Here are some suggestions:

- How To – these are among the most watched videos on the net. For a start, you can show customers how to use your product.

- Customer testimonials – this is something you should not miss.

- Vlog – thinking of writing a blog, why not make a video out of it?

Chapter 8: Podcasting

Here is the great news about podcasting: it was dead, and now it is back. For a business, this is an opportunity you shouldn't miss.

Podcasting is the process of releasing an audio series that customers can download from the internet. And once a person subscribes to your podcast, his computer downloads subsequent episodes automatically.

Why Go for Podcasting?

The decision to include podcasting in your marketing campaign is up to you. Here are some of the reasons that may inspire you to:

Podcasting is easier than video – let's face it, video isn't for everyone and this is where podcasting will save you from settling for written words only.

Podcasts give people a break – consumers want to give their eyes a break. Podcasting is facilitated by the availability of computers, mobile phones, and TVs.

Podcasts are flexible – people can listen to them while doing another task. This is impossible with videos and texts.

It builds authority – by podcasting, you will secure a place in your industry as an expert. This will build trust in your customers.

How to Get Started

There are a couple of things that will ensure a successful podcast. Here they are:

Get artwork – you have heard it before: don't judge a book by its cover. Yet we all still do it. So do yourself a favor, get artwork that is both professional and attractive.

Come up with a good name – the name of your podcast must be easy to remember and should communicate what the show is all about.

Prepare – before you begin recording, it pays to think of what you will say. So for every podcast, take time to make an outline.

Learn to edit – this will take your work from good to better. Just don't get carried away with it. A little goes a long way.

Get the necessary tools – here is a list of what you need:

- A USB microphone – for the love of Mike, stay away from your computer's built-in microphone. A USB mic is a great option; it's cheap and it produces decent results. So no excuses.

- Software – there are a couple of software packages you can use. Adobe Audition, Audacity, and Garageband are some of the most popular ones.

- A pair of headphones – this does not need to be super-duper. Anything in the $50 range should be adequate. You can upgrade later.

Chapter 9: Email Marketing

Email marketing is an old-time marketer's best friend. Despite major shifts in marketing practices, it has stood the test of time.

It refers to the process of sending commercial messages to people by email. The aim is to increase brand loyalty and recognition, increase sells, inform customers about new products, and many other reasons.

Why Bother with Email Marketing?

The long-standing popularity of email marketing is proof of its effectiveness. Here are some of its benefits:

It is targeted – you can choose the group of people to get your emails based on their characteristics. Some of the determinants can be location, gender, income range, etc. This kind of targeting ensures that the message is only seen by people likely to take the necessary action.

Easy to track – other forms of advertising, like TV or radio, are hard to track. This is not the case with email marketing.

Emails can be personalized – you can customize each email to look like it was meant for an individual - this can be more successful than sending generalized messages.

Emails are cheaper – this is among the most prominent advantages of email marketing.

How to Be Successful with Email Marketing

Just as with the other online marketing strategies, success with email marketing doesn't come easy. In the beginning, it's a lot of work, but once it's underway, things get a bit easier. However, you should not fold your arms and watch – you must monitor the results and make changes if necessary. Here are some tips you can follow:

Make your emails attractive – the heading should be attention-grabbing. Again, the colors and layout of your email must keep the reader interested. Many marketers only focus on the content of the email and not its appearance, which is a mistake.

Personalize the emails – your emails must at least address each reader with his or her name. This builds trust and is effective at making you achieve your goal.

Offer incentives – your readers are always busy. So if they take the time to do what you ask for, you must thank them. You can do this with a discount, a free download, or anything else they will value.

Send at the right time – timing matters if you want to get your emails opened. Mid-week, mid-day works pretty well. That is, you must send your emails on Tuesday, Wednesday, or Thursday around 1-3pm. You can break this rule, however, if it's necessary.

Grow your list – your email marketing campaign will fall to the ground if you do not have a list. Here is how you can grow it:

- have a signup form on your website – easy to put in place but not very effective.

- offer free stuff and get emails in exchange, e.g. eBook downloads.

- ask for emails at checkout.

- ask for emails when a customer calls in.

Chapter 10: Get Endorsements

The consumer's voice is becoming more important every day. In one research, 90% of buyers were influenced by positive reviews they read online. If you want success, testimonials are a goldmine you should ignore at your own risk.

However, this topic takes us back to Chapter 1. Great reviews will only come if your customers are satisfied. So creating high customer value is important.

How to Get Endorsements

A frustrated customer and a highly satisfied one are the only people who find it easy to review your business. Your job is to get good reviews from every part of the spectrum. Here are some tips on how you can achieve that:

Ask customers to offer reviews – the easiest way to get reviews is to ask for them. So when someone buys from you, wait for a few days before asking him to provide a review of your product. To ensure success, you must...

Make the process easy – no review is worth climbing a mountain for. An example of a hurdle is the need to register at a website before leaving a review. Instead, give your customers an option to review your business on a platform of their choice. This can be Facebook, Google places, Yahoo local, etc.

Provide incentives – there is no such thing as a free lunch. If you want reviews, provide your customers an incentive for fulfilling your wishes. Free downloads and discounts are things you can think of.

Get people to try your products – this is another popular way of getting reviews. However, the customers will have to make it clear that you offered them your product to review.

Ask for honest reviews – desist from asking customers to give you positive reviews. Instead, ask them to be as honest as possible. Buying good reviews is unethical.

Thank your reviewers – the customer took his time to review your product, so why not thank him?

Resolve grievances – negative reviews can be destructive just as positive ones can be effective. So if a customer has complained about your product, do what you can to make him happy. A review from a dissatisfied customer that states how much you care is better than a bad one.

Conclusion

I hope this book was helpful to you. Running a business requires you to take bold steps. Deciding to start using internet marketing is one such bold step.

What you must do now is to choose a few strategies you can manage to follow. When you make your selection, get the necessary materials to help you get better at the strategies you have chosen. Making it in the business environment is not easy. But if you have the guts, you can bet that you will succeed.

www.ingramcontent.com/pod-product-compliance
Lightning Source LLC
Chambersburg PA
CBHW070423190526
45169CB00003B/1386